THERE ONCE
LIMERICK ANT

Lewis Carroll, Robert Frost, Edwar
Carolyn Wells, Woodrow Wilson and Others

DOVER THRIFT EDITIONS

Edited by
Michael Croland

DOVER PUBLICATIONS
GARDEN CITY, NEW YORK

DOVER THRIFT EDITIONS

GENERAL EDITOR: SUSAN L. RATTINER
EDITOR OF THIS VOLUME: MICHAEL CROLAND

To Jack, Nancy, and Benjamin

Bibliographical Note

There Once Was a Limerick Anthology is a new work, first published by Dover
Publications in 2022.

International Standard Book Number

ISBN-13: 978-0-486-84961-4
ISBN-10: 0-486-84961-9

Manufactured in the United States of America
849619001   2022
www.doverpublications.com

Contents

Acknowledgments

The editor and the publisher are grateful for permission to include the following limericks.

"For Travelers Going Sidereal" by Robert Frost, © 1972 by the Estate of Robert Frost. Reprinted with the permission of the Robert Frost Copyright Trust.

"Decline of the West" by Fred Hornaday, © 2016 by Fred Hornaday. Reprinted with the permission of Fred Hornaday.

"When the problems of Health seem titanic" by Max Huberman, © 1964 by Max Huberman. Reprinted with the permission of Mark Huberman.

"We fight to prove we are not the same" by Cheryl Ingram, © 2020 by Cheryl Ingram. Reprinted with the permission of Cheryl Ingram, Diverse City LLC.

"Today, I ate a pupusa" by Mama Bear Gina, © 2019 by Jeanne Crowley. Reprinted with the permission of Jeanne Crowley.

Thank you to Peter Lenz, Susan Rattiner, and Andrew Sliwoski for your support of this anthology. Thank you to the rest of the Dover team, especially Peter Donahue, Janet Kopito, and Marie Zaczkiewicz.

Thank you, Eric Jonas, for fostering my interest in limericks.

Thank you to Anna Cohn Orchard, Melissa Eliot, Marco Graziosi, Grzegorz Gigol, Doug Harris, Lisa Huberman, Jonah Schrogin, and Bob Turvey for your help.

Thank you, Tamara, for your love and patience. Considering that I proposed to you with a limerick, this project wasn't unforeseeable.

Poetically speaking, here's a shout-out to Robin, Mom, Alan, Marla, Dan, Lisa, Zachary, and Zoey.

Introduction

If the Limerick's cocktail you'd quaff,
Stir nonsense and wit, each a half,
  Add a dash of good fun,
  Drop in a pun—
And then make a noise like a laugh.
                              WALLACE RICE

In its standard form, a limerick consists of a single stanza with five lines. There is an *aabba* rhyme scheme, meaning that the first, second, and fifth lines rhyme with each other and the third and fourth lines rhyme with each other. Typically, the three long *a* lines have three beats and the two short *b* lines have two beats, but there isn't a uniform number of syllables in either. The limerick's signature bouncy rhythm is called anapestic, but some poets use different rhythmic approaches.

This anthology features a variety of limericks, but most are comic in nature and focus on a single main character. In his landmark *Complete Limerick Book*, Langford Reed said that such limericks contain a cause-and-effect plot and amount to "a short story in miniature." He explained that the "leading character" should "in the first line, set out on some adventure or achievement; the second, third, and fourth lines should show the progress made, and the fifth the result." The final line should be the strongest.

Some of the best limericks depend on artful rhymes, appealing to the ear more than the eye. They flow smoothly and tell anecdotes succinctly. While some limericks embrace nonsense, many others favor wit. Limericks may appear to be straightforward, but the great ones take many considerations into account in order to pack a perfect punch. Ideally, they should make their audience laugh.

The standards for what constitutes a good limerick vary by chapter. Successful tongue twisters or limericks with creative abbreviations might not be as funny as the selections in other chapters, but they cleverly accomplish what they set out to do.

Familiarity

Limericks are familiar to us not just because of what we think of as limericks. Before limericks were named, they were sometimes called nursery rhymes, and indeed some popular nursery rhymes are in the *aabba* structure. Originally composed in French circa 1744, "Hickory, Dickory, Dock" is the best-known example:

> Hickory, dickory, dock,
> The mouse ran up the clock.
> The clock struck one,
> The mouse ran down,
> Hickory, dickory, dock.

Two stanzas from another well-known nursery rhyme use this rhyme scheme:

> What are little boys made of?
> What are little boys made of?
> Frogs and snails
> And puppy-dogs' tails,
> That's what little boys are made of.

> What are little girls made of?
> What are little girls made of?
> Sugar and spice
> And all that's nice,
> That's what little girls are made of.

The Oxford Dictionary of Nursery Rhymes includes more than a dozen other examples in the limerick structure.

"If You're Happy and You Know It" and "She'll Be Coming 'Round the Mountain" are both classic children's songs that use the *aabba* rhyme scheme. So does one of America's most beloved Christmas carols, John Henry Hopkins Jr.'s "We Three Kings of Orient Are":

> We three Kings of Orient are;
> Bearing gifts we traverse afar,
>> Field and fountain,
>> Moor and mountain,
> Following yonder star.

While these examples are not considered limericks per se, their prevalence helps explain why the limerick is so welcome among readers and listeners. We become acquainted with its rhyme scheme in childhood, and it sounds right to our ears. For some, there might be a joy in subverting a perceived juvenile form with adult content.

This anthology focuses on limericks that were deliberately written as such. However, there are other examples of poetry in the limerick structure, including several in the "Famous Authorship" chapter.

Chronology

Traces of the limerick in English date back to a song from around 1300 and a manuscript from the fourteenth century. Early examples of the limerick structure can be found in the poetry of Queen Elizabeth I, Robert Herrick, and Thomas Moore as well as in the plays of William Shakespeare.

The limerick as a stand-alone poetic form took off during its golden age, between the early 1820s and 1928. The first book of limericks, *The History of Sixteen Wonderful Old Women*, was published circa 1820, and it was followed by *Anecdotes and Adventures of Fifteen Gentlemen* in 1822; both were anonymous. Edward Lear put limericks on the map with his books in 1846 and 1872. He did not use "limerick" to describe his nonsense verse, and the word entered the English language between 1882 and 1898. There was a limerick boom in England in 1907–08, with dozens of newspapers and other publications holding limerick contests with large prizes, and advertising firms followed suit. Several notable anthologies were published in the UK and the US in the 1920s, including Langford Reed's *The Complete Limerick Book* (1924), *Carolyn Wells' Book of American Limericks* (1925), and Norman Douglas's *Some Limericks* (1928).

While this volume highlights abundant material from the golden age, it also includes predecessors and successors. Later limerick champion Morris Bishop is featured, as is one of the finest poets of the twentieth century, Robert Frost. The epilogue illuminates how the tradition continues, showcasing more recent selections and contemporary concerns.

Language

Some limerick proponents claim that it is the only well-known form of poetry that originated in English. Scholars disagree about its roots in Greek, Latin, French, and Irish, including an unestablished connection with the city of Limerick in Ireland. The limerick is primarily associated with English and has enjoyed unrivaled success in English, particularly in the UK and the US.

In *The Art of the Limerick*, Cyril Bibby explored whether the limerick had thrived in English because of a "streak of nonsensicality" that is "peculiar to English." He explained:

> I strongly suspect that certain features of the language itself have also played an important part. Its great economy allows the compression of complete statements into very short lines. Its characteristically strong stressing is suited to the oral repetition of humorous or satirical verse. Its marvelously rich and varied vocabulary facilitates the task of any versifier struggling for a third-rhyme ending to the limerick's fifth and final line.

Working within these parameters, many limericks boast an impressive vocabulary and literary merit.

Authorship

Authorship is often unclear, in part because many limericks were passed on through oral tradition. In addition, many creators did not want to besmirch their reputations by being associated with ribald content, especially when it was considered more taboo. Accordingly, limericks by renowned writers George Bernard Shaw and Alfred, Lord Tennyson, are not extant.

Most limericks are anonymous, and all unattributed poems in this volume were published by 1926. Poets' names are included if they are known.

Humor

The editor has let some "inconvenient truths" slide for the sake of a joke. Fleas and Barbary apes lack wings and tails, respectively, but these facts are overlooked.

Humor is subjective. In selecting the material, the editor favored ingenious rhymes and puns over offensive content that might have gotten a bigger laugh out of some readers.

In a bygone era, many limericks portrayed women and different races, ethnicities, and religions in a demeaning light, sometimes with appalling slurs. The implicit message was that the poets, typically white and male, could freely disparage others in the name of comedy. That approach has not stood the test of time.

This anthology steers clear of misogyny, racism, homophobia, and transphobia. Some classic limericks have been omitted. While "dame" (woman), "gay" (merry), "harlot" (prostitute), "maid" or "maiden" (unmarried girl or woman), and "wench" (young girl or woman) are loaded terms, they get a pass in limericks from yesteryear. To be sure, many selections deride individual fictional characters. However, they should not be seen as representative of their sex, nationality, or other group.

In the twenty-first century, humorists should consider the impact of their words and err on the side of caution and respect.

EDWARD LEAR

English writer and painter Edward Lear did not invent limericks. He wrote "nonsense rhymes," and his limericks are neither the most intellectual nor the most humorous. He penned limericks with four lines instead of five, with the two would-be short lines on the same line; Lear's limericks are formatted with five lines in this collection in order to be consistent with the other selections. The final line often repeats the rhyming word and other content from the first line rather than saying something new. Despite these shortcomings, Lear's creations have clever, succinct plots that amuse readers, especially their intended audience: children. They serve as a foundation for subsequent limericks. Lear has been called "The Poet Laureate of the Limerick," having popularized limericks more than any other poet.

Lear's 212 limericks were published in two different books. Standouts from both are featured. The first four limericks are from A Book of Nonsense *(1846). The next five are from* More Nonsense, Pictures, Rhymes, Botany, Etc. *(1872).*

There was an Old Man with a beard,
Who said, "It is just as I feared!—
 Two Owls and a Hen,
 Four Larks and a Wren,
Have all built their nests in my beard!"
                                        EDWARD LEAR

1

There was an old Man of th' Abruzzi,
So blind that he couldn't his foot see;
　　When they said, "That's your toe,"
　　He replied, "Is it so?"
That doubtful old Man of th' Abruzzi.
EDWARD LEAR

There was an Old Lady whose folly,
Induced her to sit in a holly;
　　Whereon by a thorn,
　　Her dress being torn,
She quickly became melancholy.
EDWARD LEAR

There was an Old Person of Cromer,
Who stood on one leg to read Homer;
　　When he found he grew stiff,
　　He jumped over the cliff,
Which concluded that Person of Cromer.
EDWARD LEAR

There was an old man of Toulouse
Who purchased a new pair of shoes;
　　When they asked, "Are they pleasant?"—
　　He said, "Not at present!"
That turbid old man of Toulouse.
EDWARD LEAR

There was a young lady of Firle,
Whose hair was addicted to curl;
　　It curled up a tree,
　　And all over the sea,
That expansive young lady of Firle.
EDWARD LEAR

There was an old person of Newry,
Whose manners were tinctured with fury;
   He tore all the rugs,
   And broke all the jugs
Within twenty miles' distance of Newry.
EDWARD LEAR

There was a young lady of Greenwich,
Whose garments were border'd with Spinach;
   But a large spotty Calf,
   Bit her shawl quite in half,
Which alarmed that young lady of Greenwich.
EDWARD LEAR

There was an old person of Minety
Who purchased five hundred and ninety
   Large apples and pears,
   Which he threw unawares,
At the heads of the people of Minety.
EDWARD LEAR

GEOGRAPHICAL LIMERICKS

The largest category of limericks is geographical limericks. The first appeared in The Midwife, or Old Woman's Magazine *around 1750. The place typically has no connection to the other content and is chosen to set up a rhyme.*

These selections encompass all six inhabited continents and beyond. Most of the other chapters include geographical limericks with a different spin.

There once was a monk of Algeria
Who of fasting grew weary and wearier—
   Till one day with a yell
   He rushed from his cell,
And swallowed his Father Superior.

A two-toothed old man of Arbroath
Gave vent to a terrible oath.
   When one chanced to ache,
   By an awful mistake
The dentist extracted them both!

There was a young woman of Ayr,
Tried to steal out of church during prayer,
    But the squeak of her shoes
    So enlivened the pews
That she sat down again in despair.

There once was a lad of Baghdad,
An inquisitive sort of a lad,
    Who said, "I will see
    If a sting has a bee."
And he very soon found that it had!

There was a young woman of Bala
Who wanted to marry a tailor;
    But the men that made clothes
    Would never propose,
So she had to make shift with a sailor.

There once was a girl in Baroda
Who liked every perfume they showed her.
    Through faulty routine
    They dispatched paraffin,
Which wasn't the odor they owed her.

There's a very mean man of Belsize,
Who thinks he is clever and wise.
    And, what do you think?
    He saves gallons of ink
By simply not dotting his "i's."

There was an old man of Blackheath,
Who sat on his set of false teeth.
    Said he, with a start,
    "O Lord, bless my heart!
I've bitten myself underneath!"

There was a young lady of Boston
Whose manner had such a deep frost on,
    She invariably froze
    Every one of her beaux
When her high plane of thought they got lost on.

An indolent vicar of Bray
His roses allowed to decay;
    His wife, more alert,
    Bought a powerful squirt,
And said to her spouse, "Let us spray."

                              LANGFORD REED

A friend of mine out in Brazil
Was scaling a tree with much skill—
    Quite a perilous climb,
    As I said at the time,
And he came down more rapidly still.

There was an old lady of Brooking,
Who had a great genius for cooking;
    She could bake sixty pies
    All of quite the same size,
And tell which was which without looking.

There was a young man of Cadiz,
Who inferred that life is what it is,
   For he early had learnt,
   If it were what it weren't,
It could not be that which it is.

There was a young lady of Cheltenham,
Put on tights just to see how she felt in 'em,
   But she said with a shout,
   "If you don't pull me out,
I'm sure I shall jolly soon melt in 'em."

A lawyer who lived in Chicago
In arguing so made his jaw go
   That when he was dead
   It still wagged in his head,
And frightened whoever it saw go!

There was a young lady of Condover,
Whose husband had ceased to be fond of her;
   He could not forget
   He had wooed a brunette,
But peroxide had now made a blonde of her.

There was a young lady of Crete,
Who was so exceedingly neat;
   When she got out of bed
   She stood on her head,
To make sure of not soiling her feet.

There was a young lady of Diss,
Who said, "Now I think skating bliss."
    But no more will she state,
    For a wheel off her skate
Made her finish up something like this.

There was an old man of Dumbarton
Whom nothing on Earth could dishearten.
    When his daughter went blind
    He said, "Never mind;
There ain't much to see in Dumbarton."

A clergyman out in Dumont
Keeps tropical fish in the font;
    Though it always surprises
    The babes he baptizes,
It seems to be just what they want.

                                        MORRIS BISHOP

There was a young fellow of Ealing,
Devoid of all delicate feeling.
    When he read, on the door,
    "Don't spit on the floor,"
He jumped up and spat on the ceiling.

There's a certain young girl of the East,
Whose extravagant ways have increased.
    She's perfectly reckless,
    Her latest new necklace—
Well, it must have cost fourpence, at least.

There was a young lady of Eden,
Who on apples was quite fond of feedin'.
   She gave one to Adam,
   Who said, "Thank you, madam."
And then both skedaddled from Eden.

There was an old woman of Filey,
Who valued old candle-ends highly;
   When no one was looking
   She used them for cooking.
"It's wicked to waste," she said dryly.

There was a young lady of Florence,
Who for kissing professed great abhorrence,
   But when she'd been kissed,
   And found what she'd missed,
She cried till the tears came in torrents.

A hair-brained galoot of Galena
Once said that no labor was meaner
   Than clearing his mind—
   'Twas suggested he find
Relief with a vacuum cleaner.

There was a young lady of Glasgow,
Whose party proved quite a fiasco.
   At nine-thirty, about,
   The lights all went out,
Through a lapse on the part of the Gas Co.

There once was a lady from Guam,
Who said, "Now the sea is so calm
   I will swim, for a lark";
   But she met with a shark.
Let us now sing the ninetieth psalm.

There was a young lady of Haddow
Who quarreled one day with her shadow;
   So in both hands she took it,
   And to fragments she shook it,
This hasty young lady of Haddow.

There was a young lady of Ham
Who hastily jumped on a tram.
   As she swiftly embarked,
   The conductor remarked,
"Your fare, miss"; she said, "Yes, I am."

There was a young man of Herne Bay,
Who was making some fireworks one day;
   But he dropped his cigar
   In the gunpowder jar.
There *was* a young man of Herne Bay.

A certain old lady of Hook
Once persuaded herself she could cook;
   But could not explain why,
   When they opened the pie,
They discovered the cookery-book.

A lady is living at Ince
Who once was engaged to a prince;
  The careless young rotter
  Completely forgot her:
She's turned a Republican since.

There was a young native of Java,
Who frequently said he would halve a
  Bold head of a neighbor
  With one stroke of his saber;
He was such an accurate carver.

There was an old person of Kars
Who longed to investigate Mars.
  He lighted a rocket
  He had in his pocket,
And hurried away to the stars.

There was a young man of Laconia,
Whose mother-in-law had pneumonia;
  He hoped for the worst,
  And after March First
They buried her 'neath a begonia.

A thoughtful old man of Lahore,
When a subject was getting a bore,
  Would wisely arrange
  Conversation to change
By falling in fits on the floor.

MRS. CHARLES HARRIS

There was an old woman of Leeds
Who spent all her life in good deeds;
   She worked for the poor
   Till her fingers were sore,
This pious old woman of Leeds.

There once was an old man of Lyme
Who married three wives at a time;
   When asked, "Why the third?"
   He replied, "One's absurd!
And bigamy, sir, is a crime."

               COSMO MONKHOUSE

There was a young lady of Lynn,
Who believed in original sin.
   She'd try to be good
   As hard as she could—
And then she'd go at it ag'in.

There was an old man of Madrid,
Who ate sixty-five eggs for a quid.
   When they asked, "Are you faint?"
   He replied, "No, I ain't,
But I don't feel as well as I did."

There was a young lady of Maine,
Who was horribly sick in the train.
   Not once, but again,
   And again, and again,
And again, and again, and AGAIN!

There was a young man of Mark Lane
Who constructed an aeroplane.
 It certainly rose
 As far as that goes,
But his tombstone was simple and plain.

There once lived a man in Mauritius
Whose nature was very suspicious.
 There was no one he'd trust,
 All the world was unjust,
And everyone equally vicious.

There was a young lady of Michigan;
To see her I never could wish again.
 She would eat ice cream
 Till with pain she would scream,
Then order another big dish again.

There was a young man of Moose Jaw,
Who wanted to see Bernard Shaw;
 When they questioned him why,
 He made no reply,
But sharpened his circular saw.

A philosopher out in Mount Holly
Writes books on the world and its folly;
 When he has to relax
 From his savage attacks,
He likes to play train with his dolly.

MORRIS BISHOP

There was a young lady of Niger,
Who smiled as she rode on a tiger;
　　They returned from the ride
　　With the lady inside,
And the smile on the face of the tiger.

A pushing young man in Patchogue
Runs a Radio Hour for the Dog.
　　His program of growls,
　　Barks, bays, whines, and howls
Is setting the dog world agog.

MORRIS BISHOP

There was a young fellow of Perth
Who was born on the day of his birth.
　　He was married, they say,
　　On his wife's wedding day,
And he died on his last day on Earth.

There was an old man of Peru,
Who found he had nothing to do.
　　So he sat on the stairs
　　And counted his hairs,
And found he had seventy-two.

There is a young man of Podunk
Whose woolen pajamas have shrunk.
　　They're getting so small,
　　He can't even crawl—
He tumbles right into his bunk.

There dwells an old man in Portsoken
Who for twenty-two years hasn't spoken.
    It has not been explained,
    But he's always maintained
A silence severe and unbroken.

There was a young lady of Rio,
Who essayed to take part in a trio;
    But her skill was so scanty
    She played it *andante*
Instead of *allegro con brio*!

A lady, residing at Rye,
I'm sorry to say, told a lie,
    When she said, while out shopping,
    "Just now I'm not shopping;
I'll come by, and buy, by and by."

There was a young swell of Saltash,
Who had been in a motoring smash.
    When, his vanity humbled,
    He pointed and mumbled,
"You've sewn up my mouth—not a gash!"

A charming old lady of Settle
Instead of a hat wore a kettle.
    When the people derided,
    Said she, "I've decided
To show all the neighbors my mettle."

There was an old maid of Shanghai,
Who was so exceedingly shy,
   When undressing at night,
   She turned out the light,
For fear of the All–Seeing Eye.

There was an old man of Sheerness,
Who invited two friends to play chess,
   But he'd lent all the pieces
   To one of his nieces,
And had stupidly lost the address.

There was an old native of Spain
Whose legs were cut off by a train.
   When his friends said, "How sad!"
   He replied, "I am glad,
For I've now lost my varicose vein."

There was a young man of St. Kitts,
Who was very much troubled with fits;
   The eclipse of the moon
   Threw him into a swoon,
When he tumbled and broke into bits.

There was an old girl of St. Pancras,
Whose temper was bitter and rancorous;
   If you ask me why
   I can only reply
That her nature was highly cantankerous.

There was a young man in St. Paul
Who fell in the spring in the fall.
    If he'd died in the spring,
    't would have been a good thing;
But he didn't—he died in the fall.

There was an old man of Tarentum
Who gnashed his false teeth till he bent 'em.
    When asked what they cost
    And how much he lost,
He said, "I don't know. I just rent 'em."

A bad-tempered bully of Thurso
Was muzzled because he would curse so.
    But the signs that resulted
    Everyone so insulted,
They cried out, "Ungag him, he's worse so!"
                                    LANGFORD REED

There was an old man of Tobago,
Long lived on rice, sugar, and sago;
    Till one day, to his bliss,
    His physician said this—
"To a leg of roast mutton you may go."

There was an old fellow of Tonga,
Who was frightened to death by a conger;
    And a medico said,
    When he found he was dead,
"What a pity his nerves were not stronger!"

There was an old lady of Tooting,
Who wanted to learn parachuting.
   Though they tried to repress her,
   She jumped from the dresser,
A perfect volplane executing.

There was a young person of Tottenham
Whose manners, Good Lord! She'd forgotten 'em.
   When she went to the vicar's,
   She took off her knickers,
Because she said she was hot in 'em.

A gentleman living in Troy
Exhibited symptoms of joy;
   Said his friends, "Goodness me!
   Why these spasms of glee?"
And the gentleman said, "It's a boy!"

There was a young lady of Truro,
Who packed all her clothes in a bureau;
   But burglars came there,
   So the poor girl must wear
The costume of Eve *in futuro*.

There was a young man of the Tyne,
Put his head on the Southeastern line;
   But he died of ennui,
   For the 5:53
Didn't come till a quarter past nine.

There was a young lady of Venice
Who used hard-boiled eggs to play tennis;
    When they said, "You are wrong,"
    She replied, "Go along!
You don't know how prolific my hen is!"

There was an old buck of Verona
Who tried a new brand of bologna,
    But the pain 'neath his belt
    Was so great that he felt
He pitied the whale more than Jonah.

There was a young man of Westphalia,
Who yearly grew tail-ier and tail-ier,
    Till he took on the shape
    Of a Barbary ape,
With the consequent paraphernalia.

There was a young chap from Woonsocket
Had money, a watch, and a locket.
    He went to the track,
    And when he got back
All he had was his fist in his pocket.

A foolish young fellow of Yarrow
Once tried to converse with a sparrow.
    When the sparrow went "squeak,"
    He said, "How you speak!
It thrills me right through to my marrow."

WHAT'S IN A NAME?

The limericks in this chapter focus on a fictional character's name rather than a location. In most cases, the setup is similar to that of geographical limericks. The selections typically begin with a variation of "There was a . . ." and give the character's name.

A young man called Alfred once said,
"Why, Gertrude, your hair is quite red."
   She replied, "Oh, you brute!"
   And smacked him, to boot—
So they parted, Gert rude and Alf red.

There is a young lady named Babbit;
When she wants anything she will grab it.
   Some people say, "O!
   That's stealing!"—But no—
It's only a strong grasping habit.

A maiden at college, named Breeze,
Weighed down by B.A.'s and M.D.'s,
   Collapsed from the strain.
   Said her doctor, "'Tis plain
You are killing yourself—by degrees!"
MRS. WARREN

There was an old lady named Elwell,
Who liked the climate of Hell well;
   She said to the D—
   I really don't see
Why property here should not sell well.

A sweet-loving urchin named Hickey
Has a far-reaching tongue that is tricky;
   Whenever he's near,
   Preserves disappear,
Though his lips don't even get sticky.

A lazy young lady named Ide
Got dizzy each morning she tried
   Walking out half a block;
   But till crow of the cock
She could polka and two-step and glide.

There is an old codger named Kane,
Whose favorite bev'rage is rain;
   From the old oaken bucket,
   Through a straw he will suck it,
And his homestead is way down in Maine.

There was a young lady named Kate,
Who was learning on rollers to skate,
   And her friends, for a game,
   Quickly gave her the name
Of "Niag'ra"—her "falls" were so "great."
R. F. WELLS

There was a young lady named Lou
Whose suitors were more than a few.
   One, specially smitten,
   Once gave her a kitten;
Said he, "I've a feline for you."

There's a sturdy old preacher named Mellish,
Whose sermons most people think hellish;
   Much less of brimstone
   And more of ozone
Is the modernized preaching they'd relish.

There was a young girl named O'Neill,
Who went up in the great Ferris wheel;
   But when halfway around
   She looked at the ground,
And it cost her an eighty-cent meal.

There was a young man named Paul
Who went to a fancy dress ball.
   He decided, for fun,
   To go dressed as a bun;
But a dog ate him up in the hall.

There once was a builder named Perk,
With preconceived notions of work;
   All day in his brain
   He built castles in Spain:
All other construction he'd shirk.

There was a young lady named Perkins,
Who had a great fondness for gherkins;
   She went to a tea
   And ate twenty-three,
Which pickled her internal workin's.

There was an old sculptor named Phidias
Whose knowledge of art was invidious.
   He carved Aphrodite
   Without any nightie—
Which startled the purely fastidious.

There was a young fellow named Phil,
Who courted a charmer named Lil;
   Then followed, of course,
   A suit for divorce,
So you see he is courting her still.

There was a young lady named Ruth,
Who had a great passion for truth.
   She said she would die
   Before she would lie,
And she died in the prime of her youth.

There was a young person called Smarty
Who sent out his cards for a party;
   So exclusive and few
   Were the friends that he knew
That no one was present but Smarty.

There was a young fellow named Tucker
Who had all his clothes of seersucker;
　　When asked, "Will they press?"
　　He replied, "More or less,
But I like them the best when they pucker."

There was a young fellow named Tuttle,
Whose ways were exceedingly subtle;
　　He thought it a bore
　　To go in the front door,
So he entered by way of the scuttle.

There was a young fellow named Weir,
Who hadn't an atom of fear;
　　He indulged a desire
　　To touch a live wire.
('Most any old line will do here!)

There was a young fellow named West,
Who dreamed he was being suppressed;
　　And when he woke up he
　　Discovered a puppy
Had fallen asleep on his chest.

An old man whose surname was White
Had whiskers that grew in the night.
　　They grew such a pace
　　That they hid all his face,
And he couldn't see when it was light.

QUOTATIONS

These limericks revolve around quotations. A sizable chunk of the limerick consists of at least one quotation. The quotations range in length from just more than two lines to the full five lines. In some cases, there is dialogue between two speakers.

An old man observed, "I agree
That people drink far too much tea.
    It's more deadly, I hear,
    Than the working man's beer
And not half so pleasant to me."

Said a man whom I asked, "What's amiss?"
"I am great on connubial bliss;
    But the trouble begins
    With the third pair of twins—
I hardly expected all this."

There's a tiresome young man in Bay Shore;
When his fiancée cried, "I adore
    The beautiful sea!"
    He replied, "I agree
It's pretty; but what is it *for?*"

MORRIS BISHOP

There was a young girl of Blackwall
Who proposed to a man at a ball.
  He said, "Oh, all right,
  You're the fifth one tonight,
And I've gone and accepted them all."

To his wife said a person named Brown,
"My dear, there's a caller from town."
  "Wait," she cried in distress,
  "Till I slip on a dress."
But she slipped on the stairs and came down.

A lady once said to me, "Can
You imagine the future of man?
  Are we dead when we die?"
  I refused to reply.
But I turned round abruptly and ran.

Said the cow as she patiently chewed,
"Latest notions I've always pursued—
  So much masticated,
  It need not be stated,
My cud becomes Fletcherized food."

A man to whom illness was chronic,
When told that he needed a tonic,
  Said, "O Doctor dear,
  Won't you please make it beer?"
"No, no," said the doc, "that's Teutonic."

A small man once started to climb
Up the tower to Big Ben, saying, "I'm
   So sorry to vex,
   But I've mislaid my specs,
And I want to see what is the time."

Said a zealous young student named Coles,
"As we always term Poland folk 'Poles,'
   I'm more than inclined,
   With my logical mind,
To designate Holland's sons 'Holes.'"
F. C. WILSON

There was an old fellow of Cosham,
Who took out his false teeth to wash 'em.
   But his wife said, "Now, Jack,
   If you don't put them back,
I'll jump on the d—— things and squash 'em."

A dude upon starting the craze,
For overcoats made of green baize,
   When asked, "Do they fit?"
   Replied, "Not a bit,
But think how the people will gaze."

There once was a skunk in the dell
Who hated all people, they tell;
   "Human beings," he said,
   Always fill me with dread,
Plus they give off that terrible smell!"
FRANK JACOBS

There was an old man who said, "Do
Tell me how I'm to add two and two?
  I'm not very sure
  That it doesn't make four—
But I fear that is almost too few."

Last week I remarked to an emu,
"I cannot pretend I esteem you.
  You're a greedy old bird
  And your walk is absurd,
But your curious feathers redeem you."

"Dear me!" said a lady who frowned.
"My husband is not to be found.
  I would give a reward
  Just to have him restored,
But I won't offer more than a pound."

To an eagle declared a giraffe,
"Soon I'll fly up and tear you in half";
  Said the eagle, up high,
  "Okay, give it a try—
It's been years since I've had a good laugh."
                                    FRANK JACOBS

Said a fervent young lady of Hammels,
"I object to humanity's trammels!
  I want to be free!
  Like a bird! Like a bee!
Oh, why am I classed with the mammals?"
                                    MORRIS BISHOP

There was an old man in a hearse,
Who murmured, "This might have been worse;
   Of course the expense
   Is simply immense,
But it doesn't come out of my purse."

Said a maiden, "It's raining; however,
To cross the main road I'll endeavor.
   It's ten inches deep,
   But it's foolish to weep,
For that makes it wetter than ever."

Said a scoundrel, "I'm lucky indeed,
As I'll be the first to concede.
   I murdered a peer,
   But from what I can hear
The jury have now disagreed."

There once was an old jelly-fish,
Who said, very sadly, "I wish
   I lived in the Red Sea,
   For then I would be
A red current jelly fish!"

Said a widower living at Lydd,
"Of my wife I am happily rid;
   And by hook or by crook
   I must write a big book
On the terrible things that she did."

A lion, while combing his mane,
Observed, "Though one may not be vain,
   When the birds of the air
   Build their nests in one's hair,
It is certainly time to complain."

A fellow once murmured, "Dear me!
My uncle has perished at sea.
   His will was quite small;
   He's left nothing at all,
And I've been appointed trustee!"

"I have heard," said a maid of Montclair,
"Opportunity's step on the stair;
   But I couldn't unlock
   To its magical knock,
For I always was washing my hair."

                  MORRIS BISHOP

Said Mrs. Isosceles Tri,
"That I'm sharp I've no wish to deny;
   But I do not dare
   To be perfectly square—
I'm sure if I did I should die!"

           CLINTON BROOKS BURGESS

There once was a centipede neat,
Who bought shoes for all of his feet;
   "For," he said, "I might chance
   To go to a dance,
And I must have my outfit complete."

There was a wise man who said, "Odd
If the Heavenly path could be trod
  By spending your cash
  Upon pleasures and trash
And not spending any on God."

There once was a man who said, "Oh,
Please, good Mr. Bear, let me go;
  Don't you think that you can?"
  The bear looked at the man,
And calmly responded, "Why, no!"

"No Hoboken ride! You must pay!"
"Syracuse me not wrongly, I pray;
  Utica ticket from me
  Back in East Tennessee.
I've no money; Pawtucket away."

There was a wise man who said, "Prayer
Is as simple as breathing the air,
  If you always recall,
  Whatsoever befall,
That your Heavenly Father is there."

There once was a pious young priest,
Who lived almost wholly on yeast;
  "For," he said, "it is plain
  We must all rise again,
And I want to get started, at least."

There was an old lady of Quetta
Who wrote to her son in a letter,
  "To gamble, my lad,
  Is both wicked and bad,
Yet if you don't bet, you're no bettor."

"With pardonable pride, I remark,
I'm a Mayflower descendant," said Clark—
  Whereat Miss Brisbayne
  Replied with disdain,
"My relations once sailed in the Ark."

There was an old man who said, "Run!
The end of the world has begun.
  If you've got no excuse,
  You'll go to the deuce;
I wouldn't say this just for fun."

There was a young lady of Ryde
Who said, "I'm cut out for a bride;
  So bring me a veil,
  And a dress with a tail,
And a man must be also supplied."

There was a young dyer of Rye
Who said, with a sorrowful sigh,
  "'Tis sad to relate,
  Yet this is my fate,
Each day that I live I must dye."

Said a man, "I was never at school;
In my spare time I learnt, as a rule."
 I thought, "This is sad—
 Not much leisure you've had,"
But to say as much would have been cruel.

Said a scholarly fellow of Siam:
"I frequently read Omar Khayyam.
 His morals depress,
 But, nevertheless,
He is nearly as clever as I am."

There was a young lady of Stornoway,
Who, by walking, her feet had all worn away.
 Said she, "I don't mind;
 I think I shall find
That I've taken that terrible corn away."

A leopard once shed a great tear,
And sighed, "Ah! My life is quite drear,
 For I am covered with lots
 Of these big ugly spots
And stripes are the fashion this year."

There was a young lady of Tenby,
Who wrote to a lady friend: "N.B.—
 Now, don't be misled,
 I don't want to wed,
But where can the eyes of the men be?"

Said a tippler while tending his thirst,
"I could swallow good beer till I burst."
    Said a temperance dame,
    "It is always the same—
The best beer is as bad as the worst."

Said a gleeful young man of Torbay,
"This is rather a red-letter day,
    For my great-uncle Herbert
    I've poisoned with sherbert,
Because he had too much to say."

Said an ardent young bridegroom named Trask,
"I will grant any boon that you ask";
    Said the bride, "Kiss me, dearie,
    Until I grow weary,"
But he died of old age at the task.

A one-day-old baby in Wallabout
Reflected: "Oh, what is it all about?
    I comprehend not
    Whence, whither, or what,
But I'm sure it is something to squall about."
                                        MORRIS BISHOP

Said a gallery boy, "I am willing
To own that this drama is thrilling.
    Four murders we've had.
    And a shipwreck—not bad.
You can't expect more for a shilling."

For comfort Sir Battersby wore
Big bustles behind and before;
   He said, "If you please,
   It eases the squeeze,
In subways, when crushed through the door."

CREATIVE MISSPELLINGS

Poetic license means that proper spellings can be discarded! These misspellings do more than just break the rules. The poets revel in the idiosyncrasies of spelling and pronunciation, showing tremendous love for the English language in order to butcher it so cleverly.

These limericks rely on a pattern. Take note of the conventionally spelled word at the end of the opening line. Then rhyme it with the similarly spelled words, which vary from dictionary-approved spellings. In most cases, the initial rhyming word gives away the pattern. If that word is an unfamiliar proper noun, keep the pattern in mind and look at its partners in rhyme.

The poem about violinist August Wilhelmj is the only selection in this volume for which multiple stanzas are included. There are numerous examples of poems with two or more stanzas in the limerick structure, but it is difficult for the poet to sustain momentum following the fifth line. This is especially true if that line is the punch line in a comic limerick, as the humor typically feels stale afterward.

An heiress of gay Abergavenny
Had offers of marriage full mavenny.
  She surveyed all the men
  Very gravely, and then
Said, "Thank you, I'm not taking avenny."

A maiden of gay Aberystwyth
Left her mark on a man she kept trystwyth—
   Vermilion streaks
    On his neck and his cheeks—
With the paint on the lips that she kystwyth.

There was a young woman from Aenos
Who came to our party as Venus.
   We told her how rude
    'Twas to come there quite nude,
And we brought her a leaf from the green-h'us.

THOMAS BAILEY ALDRICH

Whenever she looks down the aisle
She gives me a beautiful smaisle,
   And of all of her beaux,
    I am certain she sheaux
She likes me the best all the whaisle.

A needy young fellow of Alne
Had to put his best watch into palne.
   He sighed, "It is funny,
    I seem to spend money;
I had some, but now it's all galne."

There was a mechalnwick of Alnwick,
Whose opinions were anti-Germalnwick;
   So when war had begun,
    He went off with a gun—
The proportions of which were titalnwick.

Some day, ere she grows too antique,
In marriage her hand I shall sique;
 If she's not a coquette,
 Which I'd greatly regruette,
She shall share my $6 a wique.

A silly old man of Barinque
Went to float on the sea in a sinque.
 Someone said, "I should thinque
 That to float in a sinque
Would drive one to drinque, in a winque.
CAROL VOX

Said a bad little youngster named Beauchamp:
"Those jelly-tarts how shall I reauchamp?
 To my parents I'd go,
 But they always say 'No,'
No matter how much I beseauchamp."
CAROLYN WELLS

There was a young heiress of Beaulieu
Who gave herself unto yours treaulieu,
 But she's grown up so tall
 That she makes me feel small,
And I fear that I sought her undeaulieu.

There were some wise Turks on the Bosphorus
Who dealt very largely in phosphorus;
 They burned out one day,
 And they cried in dismay,
"Oh dear, what a terrible losphorus!"

A modern composer named Brahms
Caused in music the greatest of quahms—
   His themes so complex,
   Every critic would vex,
From symphonies clear up to psahms.

There is a young student at Bryn Mawr
Who intended she never should syn mawr;
   But the preacher in chapel
   Slipped up on an apple,
And she hasn't done nothin' but gryn mawr.

Said the gouty old Earl of Buccleuch,
Who wore a large Number Ten scheuch,
   "'t ain't pretty, I know,
   But behold my big tow!
What else can a poor fellow deuch?"

In cotillions they all kept her busy;
She was such a good dancer, Miss Lusy.
   She'd spin like a top
   Till she'd stop and then drop,
For it made her so awfully dusy.

There was an old man of Cantyre
Who was saved from a terrible fyre.
   When a medico said,
   "The poor fellow is dead,"
He sat up and said, "You're a lyre!"

A soloist cursed with catarrh
In an opera attempted to starrh;
   But the crowd got annoyed,
   And the hook was employed
Before she had gone very farrh.

A tourist was touring in Chile,
A country decidedly hile.
   While mopping his brow
   He said, "I'll allow
That to call this place Chile is sile."

A young lady sings in our choir
With hair that's the color of phoir.
   But her charm is unique;
   She has such a fair chique—
It is really a joy to be nhoir.

There once was a doughty old colonel
Whose language was something infolonel;
   He'd swear all the fall
   At nothing at all,
Growing worse when the weather got volonel.

He was in the artillery corps
And was really a terrible borps;
   When he company kept
   The girl always slept,
And sometimes she'd actually snorps.

OLIVER MARBLE

While watching a game of croquet,
Sam Brown chanced to stand in the wuet.
    He was struck in the eye
    By a ball that went heye,
And he wears a glass orb to this duet.

A man who lived up on the D
Remarked that he never could C
    Any good reason Y
    A yellow cat's I
So much larger at midnight should B.

A man who was deeply in debt
Said, "No matter whatever I gebt,
    My creditors claim
    A share of the same,
Which makes me discouraged, you bebt."

A baker who kneaded the dough
(That's supposed to be funny, you knough)
    Made his ten cent loaves smaller,
    Sold twelve for a dollar,
And my, how his business did grough!

There was a young servant at Drogheda,
Whose mistress had deeply annogheda.
    She proceeded to swear
    In language so rare
That afterwards no one emplogheda.
                                P. L. MANNOCK

A bibulous chap from Duquesne
Drank up a whole tub of champuesne.
  Said he with a laugh,
  As he sipped the last quaugh,
"I try to get drunk but in vuesne."

I know an old man of Durazzo;
I've never known anyone chazzo.
  From the time he's begun
  Till the moment he's done,
I can only say, "Really, is thazzo?"

There was a good Canon of Durham,
Who swallowed a hook and a worrum.
  Said the Dean to the Bishop,
  "I've brought a big fish up,
But I fear we may have to inter'm."

DEAN INGE

There was a young maiden called Eighmy,
Who was a good girl all the seighmy.
  At nine every night
  She'd kneel and recight
A little verse called "Now I leighmy."

Said a careless young smoker named Farquharson,
"I greatly dislike the new parquharson.
  In striking a match
  I set fire to a thatch.
And he threatens to charge me with arquharson."

There was an old girl of Genoa;
I blush when I think what Iowa.
   She's gone now to rest,
   Which I think's for the best;
Otherwise I would borrow Samoa.

There lives a young lady named Geoghegan;
The name is apparently Peoghegan.
   She'll be changing it Solquhoun
   For that of Colquhoun,
But the date is at present a veoghegan.

There was a young woman of Gloucester;
In a field a cow chacester and toucester.
   She was going to be wed,
   But she won't, for she's ded!
Billy Foucester, a coucester, has loucester.

A gentleman rider named Gower
Was injured in France in the wower.
   A man from Marseilles
   Said his horse ran aweilles
At the sound of the heavy guns' rower.

A very polite man named Hawarden
Went out to plant flowers in his gawarden.
   If he trod on a slug,
   A worm, or a bug,
He said: "My dear friend, I beg pawarden!"
CAROLYN WELLS

A sensible fellow named Hughes
Had an awful attack of the blughes,
   So he ate lemon pies
   Of unusual sies
And danced till he wore out his shughes.

"The Light of the World," the first hymn,
Was sung with such absence of vymn
   That the boss of the choir,
   A witty old schoir,
Said, "Turn up the 'light'; it is dymn."

A small boy who lived in Iquique
Had a voice irritatingly squique;
   When his father said, "Oil it,
   My son, or you'll spoil it,"
His retort was a trifle too chique.

A lively young girl of Kiushiu
Fell over a potful of gliu;
   When she would have arose
   She was stuck on her clothes,
And some had got into her shiu.

There was a young fellow named Knollys,
Who was fond of a good game of kbollys;
   He jumped and he ran,
   This clever young man,
And often he took pleasant kstrollys.

At the bar in the old inn at Leicester,
There's a beautiful barmaid named Heicester.
    She gave to each guest
    Only what was the buest,
And they all, with one accord, bleicester.

"But, chauffeur, we're going the limit
And a pond's right ahead of us, dimmit!"
    But the chauffeur replied:
    "You will please stay inside;
We are going so fast we shall skim it."
                                    GEORGE WARRINGTON

Said a maid, "I shall marry for lucre."
Then her ma stood right up and shuckre,
    But just the same
    When a chance came
The old dame said no word to rebuchre.

There once was a man named McVeagh,
Whose greatest delight was to seagh
    To those who asked why
    It was not spelled a-y,
Just simply, "That isn't the weagh."

There was a bold fellow named Meagher
Who inquired, "Are you going feagher?"
    I did not like his talk,
    Or his looks, or his walk,
So I said, "Only just to the ceagher."

There was a young lady named Menzies
Who said, "I can't think what this thenzies.
   Oh, yes, you may laugh,
   But it's crawled up my caugh.
It's a wasp! And how painful its stenzies!"

An athlete who lived in Milwaukee
Attempted one day to play haukee,
   But in less than a trice
   His feet left the ice
In a manner exceedingly gaukee.

Now there were two brothers, the Mohuns,
Who could whistle most beautiful tohuns;
   But they wore out their pharynx,
   Their tonsils, and larynx,
And now they both play on bassohuns.

A struggling attorney named Moore
Left the following note on his doore:
   "Will return again soon."
   He came back about noon,
And found someone had added, "What foore?"

An inquisitive maiden named Myrtle
Stuck her hand in the mouth of a tyrtle.
   They buried the hand
   In a piece of dry land,
Which helped make the soil very fyrtle.

There once was a man from Nantucket
Who kept all his cash in a bucket,
    But his daughter, named Nan,
    Ran away with a man,
And as for the bucket, Nantucket.

DAYTON VOORHEES

I sat by the side of the ocean
Tormenting myself with this nocean:
    If a ship isn't taut,
    Can she sail as she aut
With the wind and the waves in commocean?

A rare old bird is the Pelican,
His beak holds more than his belican.
    He can take in his beak
    Enough food for a week.
I'm darned if I know how the helican!

DIXON MERRITT

A young man of imposing physique
Bathed every day in a chrique!
    Till one day it ran dry,
    When he said with a sigh:
"Why the thing must have sprung a bad lique."

There was a young lady named Psyche,
Who was heard to ejaculate, "Pcryche!"
    For, when riding her pbych,
    She ran over a ptych,
And fell on some rails that were pspyche.

Said a lady of fashion in Putnam,
"These shoes! I can never unbutnam.
  It looks awful neat
  With snug shoes on your feet,
But I can't get 'em off without cutnam."
CAROL VOX

A foolish young student named Raleigh
Deserted a swift-moving traleigh
  To discover a flaw
  In Newton's First Law,
But his effort was faleigh, by galeigh.

A king who began on his reign
Exclaimed with a feeling of peign,
  "Though I'm legally heir,
  No one seems to ceir
That I haven't been born with a breign."

An unskhyllful rider from Rhyl
Motorcycled full-speed down a hyll,
  Thyll a spyll at a bend
  Khylled our whyllful young friend,
And he now in the churchyard lies sthyll!

Last Sunday she wore a new sacque,
Low-cut at the front and the bacque,
  And a lovely bouquet
  Worn in such a cute wuet
As only few girls have the knacque.

A pleasant young fellow named Seixas
Was thought to be rather audeixas
  Till he saw a white post
  Which he took for a gost
And ran away, screaming "Good Greixas!"

A thrifty young fellow of Shoreham
Made brown paper trousers and woreham;
  He looked nice and neat
  Till he bent in the street
To pick up a pin, then he toreham.

A lady, an expert on skis,
Went out with a man who said, "Plis,
  On the next precipice
  Will you give me a kice?"
She said, "Quick! Before somebody sis."

There was a young lady of Slough,
Who went for a ride on a cough.
  The brute pitched her off
  When she started to coff;
She ne'er rides on such animals nough.
                       LANGFORD REED

A sporty young man in St. Pierre
Had a sweetheart and oft went to sierre.
  She was Gladys by name,
  And one time when he came
Her mother said: "Gladys St. Hierre."
                FERDINAND G. CHRISTGAU

Some charming selections from Strauss
A pianist played at our hauss;
   Though we shouted "Encore!"
   And clamored for more,
The neighbors did nothing but grauss.

Two gluttonous youngsters of Streatham
Bought fifty-five doughnuts and eatham.
   The coroner said,
   "No wonder they're dead;
How unwise of their parents to leatham!"

Said a man to his wife, down in Sydenham,
"My best trousers—where have you hydenham?
   It is perfectly true
   That they weren't very new,
But I foolishly left half-a-quidenham."
                        P. L. MANNOCK

There was a young lady from Tampa
Who played a mean trick on her grampa.
   This naughty granddaughter
   Filled his slippers with waughter,
And grampa grew dampa and dampa.
                        CAROL VOX

A lady who lived by the Thames
Had a gorgeous collection of ghames.
   She had them reset
   In a large coronet
And a number of small diadhames.
                        CAROLYN WELLS

A fellow who thought he was tough
Took a poke at a pugilist rough.
  From the rents in his clothes
  And the shape of his nothes,
It was thought he had met a rebough.

There was a young lady of Twickenham,
Whose boots were too tight to walk quickenham.
  She bore them awhile,
  But at last, at a stile,
She pulled them both off and was sickenham.

There once was a party named Vaughan
Who used to incessantly yaughan;
  When they said, "It won't do,"
  He replied, "So would you
If you had to get up before daughan."

There was a young lady of Warwick
Who lived in a castle histarwick.
  On the damp castle mould
  She contracted a could,
And the doctor prescribed paregarwick.

There was a young lady named Wemyss,
Who, it semyss, was troubled with dremyss.
  She would wake in the night,
  And, in terrible fright,
Shake the bemyss of the house with her scremyss.

Oh, King of the fiddle, Wilhelmj,
If truly you love me just tellmj;
   Just answer my sigh
   By a glance of your eye,
Be honest, and don't try to sellmj.

With rapture your music did thrillmj,
With pleasure supreme it did fillmj,
   And if I could believe
   That you meant to deceive,
Wilhelmj, I think it would kilmj!

                        ROBERT J. BURDETTE

An old lady living in Worcester
Had a gift of a handsome young rorcester;
   But the way that it crough,
   As 'twould never get through,
Was more than the lady was uorcester.

A man who was steering a yacht
His course through the water forgacht.
   And he stuck in the mud
   With a dull, sick'ning thud,
And the captain then swore a whole lacht.

A man had a cow he called Zephyr;
He thought her an amiable hephyr.
   But when he drew near
   She kicked off his ear,
And now the old man is much dephyr.

CREATIVE ABBREVIATIONS

These limericks use patterns based on creative abbreviations. It may be challenging to sound out some of them on your first attempt. Pronounce the first abbreviation in the standard manner. Then apply the same pronunciation to made-up abbreviations that rhyme with the first.

There was a young man had a bro.,
Son of the father and mo.,
  Who was also a twin;
  And 't was really a sin,
For you couldn't tell one from the o.

A young lady in Wilmington, Del.,
Of the latest French fashions was wel.
  "For the outside, you see,
  They look fine, but," said she,
"I would rat. Del. und."

There once was a young lady Dr.,
Who owned a bad parrot that mr.;
   He would likewise blaspheme,
   Using language extreme—
All of which, so the lady said, shr.

When writing to J. Jones, Esq.,
Address him like that, by des.
   He likes it that way;
   But be that as it may
He's a fellow to know and adm.

There was once a maiden in Fla.
Who had no fall hat, so she ba.
   Little old bonnet;
   Men doted uponnet,
But the girls said she couldn't look ha.

A musical lady from Ga.
Once sang in "Lucretia Ba."
   Said a friend the next day,
   "I'm sorry to say
That high note in C major fla."

A young man, whose first name was Geo.,
Once ventured his pa's check to feo.;
   But they quickly found out
   What this youth was about,
And compelled him at once to disgeo.

A farmer in Knox, Ind.,
Had a daughter he called Mar.
   But the neighbors said "O,
   We really must go,"
Whenever she played the p.

A person who signs himself Jas.
Keeps a number of cats that he tas.
   To do certain tricks
   With hoops, barrels, and sticks,
Though the neighbors keep calling him nas.

In the bright Lexington of Ky.
Lives a fellow exceeding ply.
   He's going to propose
   To a rich girl he knows,
And if she says yes he'll be ly.

Upon the piano she lbs.
And makes the most deafening sbs.
   And the uproar that reigns,
   The policeman compleigns,
Keeps him nightly awake on his rbs.

If a lawyer's a LL.D.,
Then a dentist's a JJ.D.
   But it's simply absurd
   If you say of a bird
That a crow is a CC.D.

An amorous M. A.
Says that Cupid, the C. D.,
   Doesn't cast for his health
   But is rolling in wealth—
He's the John Jaco-B. H.

There once was a fiery young Maj.
Who tossed with a bull for a waj.
   When he woke in the ward
   There were none to applard;
Now that Maj. I'll waj. is saj.

A cobbler who also sold mdse.
Cut birch wood to make him some bdse.
   But the first die he cast
   Was the shoemaker's last—
He grips at his heart, gives a ldse.

There was a young lady of Me.,
Who was of her beauty quite ve.,
   But a freckle or two
   Later on came in view,
And drove the young lady inse.

A lady who lived in Mont.
Had a beautiful daughter named H.,
   Who once took a seat
   On Twentieth Street,
Having slipped on a piece of ban.

She was peeved and called him "Mr."
Not because he went and kr.,
   But because, just before,
   As she opened the door,
This same Mr. kr. sr.

There once was a widowed young Mrs.,
Who perceived no enjoyment in krs.
   An adjacent young Mr.
   Rose right up and kr.,
And she said, "Of all blrs., why, thrs.!"

When you think of the hosts without No.
Who are slain by the deadly cuco.,
   It's quite a mistake
   Of such food to partake;
It results in a permanent slo.

There is an old cook in N.Y.,
Who insists you should always st. p.
   Full vainly he's tried
   To eat some that was fried,
And says he would rather ch. c.

As he filled up the order book pp.,
He said, "I should get higher ww."
   So he struck for more pay,
   But, alas, now they say,
He is driving Fifth Avenue stst.

A cheery old learned prof.
Is the happy, contented poss.
    Of a long piece of cane,
    With which, now and again,
He still punishes any transgr.

The sermon our pastor Rt. Rev.
Began, may have had a Rt. clev.,
    But his talk, though consistent,
    Kept the end so far distant,
We left since we felt he mt. nev.

Jones had a night out in Sept.;
The rest he could never rem.
    It turned to Oct.
    Before he was s.,
But he felt quite himself in Nov.

There is a young woman in Tex.;
The whole reading world she perplex.,
    For she wrote a nice book
    Which the publishers took
For a psychical problem of sex.

There was a young maid of Wyo.,
Who liked to walk out in the glo.
    If a friend, as she passed,
    Quite politely would ask
What she'd have, she'd reply: "Something fo."

TONGUE TWISTERS

The limerick's limited real estate, intrinsic rhyme scheme, and penchant for puns invite tongue twisters. One of the most popular tongue twisters, about a woodchuck, has been adapted as a limerick.

Carolyn Wells is tied with Edward Lear for the most limericks in this anthology, and the majority appear in this chapter. In 1925, she published Carolyn Wells' Book of American Limericks, *an outstanding collection that yielded many of the limericks in this volume.*

A certain young fellow named Beebee
Wished to wed with a lady named Phoebe.
   "But," said he, "I must see
   What the clerical fee
Be before Phoebe be Phoebe Beebee."

A canner, exceedingly canny,
One morning remarked to his granny,
   "A canner can can
   Anything that he can,
But a canner can't can a can, can he?"

CAROLYN WELLS

A sawyer named Esau, from Dee,
Saw a couple see-sawing; said he
　　To his girl, "Let us see-saw!"
　　Said she, "Oh no, Esau!
See-sawing is vulgar. See! See!"

EDWARD MILLIGAN

There was a young fellow named Fisher
Who was fishing for fish in a fissure,
　　When a cod with a grin
　　Pulled the fisherman in;
Now they're fishing the fissure for Fisher.

A fly and a flea in a flue
Were imprisoned, so what could they do?
　　Said the fly, "Let us flee!"
　　"Let us fly!" said the flea.
So they flew through a flaw in the flue.

A tutor who tooted the flute
Tried to tutor two tooters to toot.
　　Said the two to the tutor,
　　"Is it harder to toot or
To tutor two tooters to toot?"

CAROLYN WELLS

'Tis said, woman loves not her lover
So much as she loves his love of her;
　　Then loves she her lover
　　For love of her lover,
Or love of her love of her lover?

There's a woman called Madame Tussaud;
Slow sewers she shows how to sew.
　　She says, "If, So-and-so,
　　You sew so, you'll sew slow,
And you'll only sew so-so. Sew so."

"There's a train at 4:04," said Miss Jenny,
"Four tickets I'll take; have you any?"
　　Said the man at the door,
　　"Not four for 4:04,
For four for 4:04 is too many!"

CAROLYN WELLS

A tailor of highest repute
Made a suit for a suitor of Butte.
　　But when donned the suit parted;
　　The suitor then started
A suit, for the suit didn't suit.

A pseudo big chief of the Sioux
Sued hard for the hand of sweet Sue;
　　He carried the day,
　　And the marriage, they say,
Of Sue and the Sioux will ensue.

There was a young fellow named Tait,
Who dined with his girl at 8:08;
　　But I'd hate to relate
　　What that fellow named Tait
And his tête-à-tête ate at 8:08!

CAROLYN WELLS

Said a wag to a farmer of Tamworth,
"What's a ram and a dam and a lamb worth?
    If the ram of a lamb
    Is not worth a dam,
What's the lamb of a ram and a dam worth?"

A fellow who slaughtered two toucans
Said, "I shall put them into two cans."
    Two canners who heard
    Said, "You'll be a bird,
If you can put two toucans in two cans."

There was a young man of Typhoo
Who wanted to catch the 2:02,
    But his friend said, "Don't hurry
    Or worry or flurry,
It's a minute or two to 2:02."

                                    CAROLYN WELLS

The bottle of perfume that Willie sent
Was highly displeasing to Millicent;
    Her thanks were so cold—
    They quarreled, I'm told,
Through that silly scent Willie sent Millicent.

A woodchuck would chuck him some wood—
He would chuck all the wood that he could;
    But the question arose:
    How much, d' you suppose
A woodchuck would chuck, if he should.

A right-handed fellow named Wright
In writing "write" always wrote "rite"
　Where he meant to write right.
　If he'd written "write" right,
Wright would not have wrought rot writing "rite."

One day I went out to the Zoo,
For I wanted to see the old Gnu,
　But the old Gnu was dead,
　They had a new Gnu instead,
And that Gnu, well he knew he was new.

G. T. JOHNSON

FAMOUS AUTHORSHIP

Numerous renowned people have penned limericks. In the US, they include President Woodrow Wilson, President George H.W. Bush, and Joseph Kennedy, the father of President John F. Kennedy. At a conference in 1990, Bush got bored and wrote dirty limericks about world leaders; his chief of staff destroyed the notes containing the limericks. In the UK, Queen Elizabeth I, Prime Minister Clement Attlee, and Prime Minister Boris Johnson have composed limericks. Johnson's won a "most offensive" poetry contest in 2016 and is not fit for print.

An all-star cast of poets and other writers is featured. William Shakespeare has been called the best dramatist of all time, and Mark Twain has been dubbed America's greatest humorist. John Galsworthy and Rudyard Kipling both won Nobel Prizes in Literature, and Robert Frost received four Pulitzer Prizes for Poetry.

Some of these limericks are excerpted from larger works, including Othello *by Shakespeare and* Ruddigore *by W. S. Gilbert, and did not originate as stand-alone limericks.*

The selections by Patrick Brontë, Queen Elizabeth I, and Shakespeare do not perfectly adhere to later conventions for limericks. Nevertheless, they demonstrate that the limerick structure has been around for a long while.

Few thought he was even a starter,
There were many who thought themselves smarter;
   But he ended PM,
   CH and OM,
An Earl and a Knight of the Garter.

CLEMENT ATTLEE

There was a young man of Montrose,
Who had pockets in none of his clothes.
  When asked by his lass
  Where he carried his brass,
He said, "Darling, I pay through the nose."
                              ARNOLD BENNETT

A spelling reformer indicted
For fudge, was before the court cited.
  The judge said: "Enough!
  Your candle we'll snough,
His sepulchre shall not be wighted."
                              AMBROSE BIERCE

Aloft on the brow of a mountain,
And hard by a clear running fountain
  In neat little cot,
  Content with her lot,
Retired, there lives a sweet maiden.
                              PATRICK BRONTË

There was a young lady of station.
"I love man" was her exclamation,
  But when men cried: "You flatter!"
  She replied: "Oh, no matter!"
"Isle of Man" is the explanation.
                              LEWIS CARROLL

There was a young lady of Whitby,
Who had the bad luck to be bit by
  Two brown little things
  Without any wings,
And now she's uncomfy to sit by.
                              LEWIS CARROLL

A charming young lady named Nelly
Once danced herself almost to jelly;
   The doctors declared
   That her life might be spared
If she stayed for a week at Pwllheli.

CHARLES COBORN

There was a brave knight of Lorraine,
Who hated to give people pain;
   "I'll skeer 'em," he said,
   "But I won't kill 'em dead!"
This noble young knight of Lorraine.

MARY MAPES DODGE

The daughter of debate
Who discord aye doth sow,
   Hath reaped no gain
   Where former reign
Hath taught still peace to grow.

QUEEN ELIZABETH I

For travelers going sidereal
The danger they say is bacterial.
   I don't know the pattern
   On Mars or on Saturn
But on Venus it must be venereal.

ROBERT FROST

An angry young husband called Bicket
Said: "Turn yourself round and I'll kick it;
   You have painted my wife
   In the nude to the life.
Do you think, Mr. Greene, it was cricket?"

JOHN GALSWORTHY

If you wish in this world to advance,
Your merits you're bound to enhance;
   You must stir it and stump it,
   And blow your own trumpet,
Or, trust me, you haven't a chance!

W. S. GILBERT

There was a Professor called Chesterton,
Who went for a walk with his best shirt on.
   Being hungry he ate it,
   But lived to regret it,
As it ruined for life his digesterton.

W. S. GILBERT

Jane is a Girle that's prittie;
Jane is a wench that's wittie;
   Yet, who wo'd think
   Her breath do's stink,
As so it doth? that's pittie.

ROBERT HERRICK

The Reverend Henry Ward Beecher
Called a hen a most elegant creature.
   The hen, pleased with that,
   Laid an egg in his hat,
And thus did the hen reward Beecher!

OLIVER WENDELL HOLMES

There's a ponderous pundit MacHugh
Who wears goggles of ebony hue.
   As he mostly sees double
   To wear them why trouble?
I can't see the Joe Miller. Can you?

JAMES JOYCE

Says the Frenchman, "You'll pay us for sure,"
Says the German, "We can't for we're poor."
    So Fritz with a whine
    Sings his "Watch on the Rhine,"
But the Poilu sings, "Watch on the Ruhr."

JOSEPH KENNEDY

A poodle was charged by the law
With resembling Hall Caine. With his paw
    Pressed close to his forehead,
    He sobbed, "Yes, it's horrid,
But at least I'm not like Bernard Shaw!"

COULSON KERNAHAN

There was a young boy of Quebec,
Who fell into the ice to his neck.
    When asked, "Are you friz?"
    He replied, "Yes, I is,
But we don't call this cold in Quebec."

RUDYARD KIPLING

There was a young lady of Limerick,
Who stole from a farmer named Tim a rick;
    When the priest at the altar
    Suggested a halter,
She fled from the county of Limerick.

ANDREW LANG

Though wisdom oft has sought me,
I scorned the lore she brought me;
    My only books
    Were women's looks,
And folly's all they've taught me.

THOMAS MOORE

The time I've lost in wooing,
In watching and pursuing,
　The light that lies
　In women's eyes
Has been my heart's undoing.

THOMAS MOORE

There's an Irishman, Arthur O'Shaughnessy—
On the chessboard of poets a pawn is he;
　Though a bishop or king
　Would be rather the thing
To the fancy of Arthur O'Shaughnessy.

DANTE GABRIEL ROSSETTI

There was a young lady of Prague,
Who was both absent-minded and vague,
　Two faults she ascribed
　To the fact she imbibed,
And her early attacks of the ague.

ATHENE SEYLER

And let me the canakin clink, clink;
And let me the canakin clink;
　A soldier's a man;
　Oh, man's life's but a span;
Why, then, let a soldier drink.

WILLIAM SHAKESPEARE

There was an old man of the Cape,
Who made himself garments of crêpe.
　When asked, "Do they tear?"
　He replied, "Here and there,
But they're perfectly splendid for shape!"

ROBERT LOUIS STEVENSON

A man hired by John Smith and Co.
Loudly declared he would tho.
   Man that he saw
   Dumping dirt near his store.
The drivers, therefore, didn't do.
                      MARK TWAIN

I sat next to the Duchess at tea;
It was just as I feared it would be:
   Her rumblings abdominal
   Were truly phenomenal,
And everyone thought it was me!
                  WOODROW WILSON

BAWDY LIMERICKS

Humorist Don Marquis quipped that limericks that could be told around "ladies" or "the clergy" were worth $1 or $2, respectively. "LIMERICKS," on the other hand, were worth $10. Many aficionados of the craft would say that a proper limerick should be improper.

These bawdy limericks rely on some standards of decency. Sexual acts involving multiple people must be consensual. The most offensive curses are avoided. Misogyny, racism, homophobia, and transphobia are eschewed. What's left is lewdness that will satisfy readers who crave vulgar humor—and disgust those who do not.

One work-around to the restrictions is to let a woman have the final say or last laugh. Another is to focus on sexual acts involving only one person. Yet another is to employ toilet humor.

There was an old man of Connaught
Whose prick was remarkably short.
  When he got into bed
  The old woman said,
"This isn't a prick; it's a wart."

There was a young parson of Goring
Who made a small hole in the flooring.
  He lined it all round,
  Then laid on the ground,
And declared it was cheaper than whoring.

There was a young parson of Harwich,
Tried to grind his betrothed in a carriage.
　　She said, "No, you young goose,
　　Just try self-abuse.
And the other we'll try after marriage."

There was a young lady named Hitchin
Who was scratching her crotch in the kitchen.
　　Her mother said, "Rose,
　　It's the crabs, I suppose."
She said, "Yes, and the buggers are itchin'."

There was an old parson of Lundy,
Fell asleep in his vestry on Sunday.
　　He awoke with a scream:
　　"What, another wet dream!
This comes of not frigging since Monday."

There was an Old Man of the Mountain
Who frigged himself into a fountain.
　　Fifteen times had he spent;
　　Still he wasn't content—
He simply got tired of the counting.

There was a young man of Rangoon
Who farted and filled a balloon.
　　The balloon went so high
　　That it stuck in the sky,
And stank out the Man in the Moon.

There was a young Royal Marine
Who tried to fart "God Save the Queen."
　　When he reached the soprano
　　Out came the guano,
And his breeches weren't fit to be seen.

There was a young man of St. Paul's
Possessed the most useless of balls.
　　Till at last, at the Strand,
　　He managed a stand,
And tossed himself off in the stalls.

There was a young girl of Uttoxeter,
And all the young men shook their cocks at her.
　　From one of these cocks
　　She contracted the pox,
And she poxed all the cocks in Uttoxeter.

There was an old harlot of Wick
Who was sucking a coal heaver's prick.
　　She said, "I don't mind
　　The coal dust and grime,
But the smell of your balls makes me sick."

MISCELLANY

Not every limerick fits into the preceding categories. Some of the best limericks do not. They can depict anthropomorphized animals or realistic situations. They can be nonsense verse in the vein of Edward Lear, or they can be cerebral or even pious. Within the familiar aabba structure, the possibilities are endless.

A man whom I know and abominate
Will sing any song that you nominate.
   He's a very deep bass;
   When he opens his face
A rasping noise seems to predominate.

In the forest an old armadillo
Took a nap 'neath a large weeping willow;
   Just a moment ago
   He learned to his woe
That a porcupine's not a good pillow.
FRANK JACOBS

By adopting a popular attitude,
With a motto that's purely a platitude,
  You may achieve fame,
  But you'll find that your name
Will never be mentioned with gratitude.

My sympathy goes to Aunt Emma;
I think it is rash to condemn her.
  With a policeman she jested,
  And then was arrested—
A rather unpleasant dilemma.

When the cornet I started to blow,
The neighbors grew peevish, you know.
  They all disapproved,
  But I'm glad they've all moved,
For the fools interrupted me so.

An elephant lay in his bunk;
In slumber his chest rose and sunk.
  He snored and he snored
  Till the jungle folks roared—
Then his wife tied a knot in his trunk.

A wonderful man in a cap
Would never use compass or map;
  His way home he found
  With his nose to the ground,
And his ears very slowly would flap.

There once was a corpulent carp
Who wanted to play on a harp;
   But to his chagrin
   So short was his fin,
He couldn't reach up to C sharp.

A person who frequently chose
To sleep standing up on his nose,
   When asked for a reason,
   Said he thus got a season
Of very delicious repose.

There was a young man from the city,
Who met what he thought was a kitty;
   He gave it a pat,
   And said, "Nice little cat!"
And they buried his clothes out of pity.

A goddess, capricious, is Fame;
You may strive to make noted your name
   But she either neglects you
   Or coolly selects you
For laurels distinct from your aim.

LANGFORD REED

No matter how grouchy you're feeling,
You'll find the smile more or less healing.
   It grows in a wreath
   All around the front teeth,
Thus preserving the face from congealing.

ANTHONY EUWER

I wish that my Room had a Floor;
I don't so much care for a Door,
  But this walking around
  Without touching the ground
Is getting to be quite a bore!

                    GELETT BURGESS

Conversation that sparkles we get
From Miss Dazzle, whose front teeth are set
  With all that she owns
  Of rare precious stones—
But in smiling she's more brilliant yet.

There was a young man who would growl
When the visiting team made a foul;
  But if during the game
  The home team did the same
He would utter a jubilant howl.

There once was an Ichthyosaurus
Who lived when the Earth was all porous;
  When he first heard his name,
  He fainted with shame,
And departed long ages before us!

Blasé Mr. Buck is imbued
With fear that his life is hoodooed:
  Though his meals are the best,
  Just now he's distressed,
That there's nothing to eat but just food.

There once was a concert and in it
Miss Lovejoy was asked to begin it.
　"About what shall I sing?"
　Asked the singer smiling;
Said a voice, "About a half minute."

Saw an epitaph—don't know who writ it—
On a tombstone intended to fit it;
　"Just Sleeping," it read.
　When I saw it I said,
"Gee whizz, when I'm dead I'll admit it!"

JOSEPH KENNETH MORT

Although at the Lim'ricks of Lear
We may feel a temptation to sneer,
　We should never forget
　That we owe him a debt
For his work as the first pioneer.

LANGFORD REED

There once were some learned M.D.'s,
Who captured some germs of disease
　And infected a train,
　Which, without causing pain,
Allowed one to catch it with ease.

OLIVER HERFORD

The limerick's furtive and mean;
You must keep her in close quarantine,
　Or she sneaks to the slums,
　And promptly becomes
Disorderly, drunk, and obscene.

MORRIS BISHOP

A clever young architect once
Thought he'd do some original stunts;
   And he got so uplifted
   His buildings all shifted
Their backs clear around to their fronts.

                OLIVER MARBLE

There was an old man in a pie.
Who said, "I must fly! I must fly!"
   When they said, "You can't do it!"
   He replied that he knew it.
But he *had* to get out of that pie!

                CAROLYN WELLS

A man who is lacking in pride
Goes to funerals far, near, and wide;
   When they ask, "Who is dead?"
   He shakes his old head:
"I dunno—I just come for the ride."

His name I can hardly recall,
But he fell off a very high wall;
   And his wife, it's believed,
   Very bitterly grieved
Because black didn't suit her at all.

I sell the best brandy and sherry
To make good customers merry;
   But at times their finances
   Run short, as it chances,
And then I feel very sad, very.

                JOHN O'TUOMY

You shall trust the Lord God from the start
With your life and your mind and your heart
   Till you come, in His strength,
   To know fully at length
Him whom now you know only in part.

Tut-Ankh-Amen, best known as old Tankh,
Was a Pharaoh of infinite rank,
   But his sarcophagus
   Wouldn't cause all this fuss
If his name had been Freddie or Frank.

ELSIE RIDGEWELL

To compose a sonata to-day,
Don't proceed in the old-fashioned way:
   Take your seat *on* the keys,
   Bump about as you please.
"Oh how modern!" the critics will say.

F. E. GLADSTONE

I'd rather have fingers than toes,
I'd rather have ears than a nose,
   And, as for my hair,
   I'm glad it's all there—
I'll be awfully sad when it goes.

GELETT BURGESS

EPILOGUE: THE TRADITION CONTINUES

Poets continue to adapt the limerick to contemporary circumstances. While this anthology has focused on classic limericks from yesteryear, the tradition lives on.

The content might be lighthearted, as seen in the examples showcasing Spanglish—a mix of Spanish and English—and mentioning the world's greatest dance. Some poets address serious matters, such as organic food and diversity. The final limerick comes from the internet's King of Limericks, who embraces sophisticated content.

Today, I ate a pupusa.
Se calló onto my blusa.
   I cried for a while,
    Then threw it on the pile.
¡Toda mi ropa está sucia!

MAMA BEAR GINA
(JEANNE CROWLEY)

A dashing young spotted hyena
Made a date with an aardvark named Lena.
   "Let's go dancing," said he;
    "Sounds like fun," answered she,
"But I won't do that darned Macarena!"

FRANK JACOBS

When the problems of Health seem titanic,
There's really no need that you panic—
    For health that will flourish,
    Eat foods that will nourish
And make sure the food is Organic.

MAX HUBERMAN

We fight to prove we are not the same;
Give differences respect, not shame.
    Diversity's great;
    Inclusion trumps hate,
And fairness is the light for your flame.

CHERYL INGRAM

Our standard of living has never been higher
You call it success and I call you a liar
    Just look what's in store
    And you'll always want more
When you're stuck in a state of relentless desire

FRED HORNADAY

SELECTED BIBLIOGRAPHY

Baring-Gould, William S. *The Lure of the Limerick: An Uninhibited History*. New York: Clarkson N. Potter, Inc., 1967.

Bishop, Morris. *Spilt Milk*. New York: G. P. Putnam's Sons, 1942.

Cerf, Bennett. *Bennett Cerf's Out on a Limerick: A Collection of Over 300 of the World's Best Printable Limericks, Assembled, Revised, Dry-Cleaned, and Annotated by Mister Cerf*. New York: Harper & Brothers Publishers, 1960.

Deex, Arthur, ed. *The Pentatette*. Monthly newsletter published by the Limerick Special Interest Group.

Huberman, Max. *Health Limericks*. Atlanta, TX: Natural Food Associates, Inc., 1964.

Jackson, Holbrook, ed. *The Complete Nonsense of Edward Lear*. 1947. Reprint, New York: Dover Publications, 1951.

Jacobs, Frank. *Looney Limericks*. Mineola, NY: Dover Publications, 1999.

Likewise Limericks. Boston: The Carol Press, 1910.

Limericks. Edison, NJ: Castle Books, 1992.

Mama Bear Gina [Jeanne Crowley]. *Lots of Limericks Quintillas Cómicas: Silly Poems in English Spanish "Spanglish."* Bloomington, IN: iUniverse, 2019. Kindle.

Opie, Iona, and Peter Opie, eds. *The Oxford Dictionary of Nursery Rhymes*. New ed. Oxford: Oxford University Press, 1997.

Parrott, E. O., ed. *The Penguin Book of Limericks*. London: Penguin Books, 1983.

Reed, Langford. *The Complete Limerick Book: The Origin, History and Achievements of the Limerick, with Over 400 Selected Examples*. New York: G. P. Putnam's Sons, 1925.

Rees, Glyn, ed. *The Mammoth Book of Limericks*. London: Robinson, 2008.

Rice, Wallace, and Francis Rice, eds. *The Little Book of Limericks*. Chicago: The Reilly & Britton Co., 1910.

Robbins, F. N. *The "Willie Ballads" with Other Limericks and Nonsense Rhymes*. Columbia, SC: The R. L. Bryan Company, 1904.

The Smile on the Face of the Tiger: A Collection of Limericks. Boston: Bacon and Brown, 1908.

Vaughn, Stanton, ed. *700 Limerick Lyrics: A Collection of Choice Humorous Versifications*. New York: Carey–Stafford Co., 1906.

Vox, Carol [William Houghton Sprague Pearce]. *The Sphinx and the Mummy: A Book of Limericks*. New York: H. M. Caldwell Co., 1909.

Washburn, William Lewis. *A Bouquet of Choice Limericks: Garnered from Various Sources and Printed for the Edification & Amusement of Lovers of This Form of Verse*. Audubon, NJ: The Palmetto Press, 1926.

Wells, Carolyn. *The Book of Humorous Verse*. New York: George H. Doran Company, 1920.

Wells, Carolyn. *Carolyn Wells' Book of American Limericks*. New York: G. P. Putnam's Sons, 1925.

Wells, Carolyn. *A Whimsey Anthology*. New York: Charles Scribner's Sons, 1906.

Wind, Augusta. *The Blew Book*. Boston: The Ball Publishing Co., 1911.

Woodward, Fred E. *Line Lost Limericks: A Guest Book*. New York: The Platt & Peck Co., 1915.